LORETTA SANTINI

FLORENCE

CRADLE OF THE ITALIAN ART

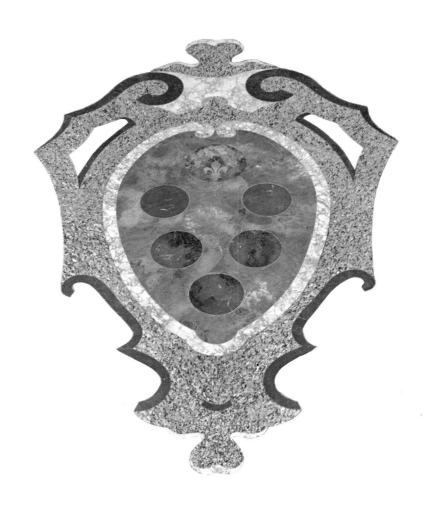

NOVA LVX
Esclusivista di vendita
per la Toscana
GIUSTI DI BECOCCI
Via Canto de' Nelli - tel. 212478
FIRENZE

INDEX

FLORENCE

The visitor to Florence, whether he looks at the Museums, Galleries, Palaces and Churches one by one, or whether he only gives a hasty glance at its most famous monuments, will always preserve in his mind the most beutiful images of the City of the Lily. They will always pass before our eyes as a sequence of treasures and masterpieces full of art, history and life.

The aim of this illustrated Album is to fix the image of Florence in few, but meaningful pictures, to gather, one by one, the highlights of its artistic life, and offer to the City a tribute to its beauty.

In compiling this illustrated Guide, our aim has always been to enable tourist to obtain in a short time a great deal of informations to serve above all in helping him to find his way among the masterpieces and art treasures to be found in Florence, where every street and square in the old centre brings to life again, unchanged, the medieval period and the splendour of the Renaissance.

We therefore decided to give only the most important data, leaving aside thel long lists of historical and artistic details. Only the most outstanding of the countless marvellous works of art to be found in the Museums and Galleries are mentioned here, with the names of the greatest artists, but in such a way as to give a clear idea of their importance. We do not pretend to have provided a history of this magnificent City, tre cradle of Italian art and civilisation, for that, would have required several volumes: instead, we have produced a practical guide, easy to consult and yet providing all the informations required.

This book, by following an ideal itinerary that unwinds from the historic centre of the city to the most interesting points of the outskirts, will be able to guide the tourist during his visit to Florence.

The Cathedral

THE CATHEDRAL, or Santa Maria del Fiore — The marvellous Cathedral, the third largest in the world, was designed in 1296 by Arnolfio di Cambio in the Tuscan Gothic style. After his death, the work was continued by Giotto, who started on the most beautiful Campanile, and Francesco Talenti, who changed Arnolfo's plan, above all by increasing the dimensions of the building.

Between 1420 and 1434, Filippo Brunelleschi, the winner of a special competition held in 1418, undertook the building of the Cupola; this was a very daring achievement, since the vault was constructed without a fixed framework.

In 1436, the building of Santa Maria del Fiore was practically completed, and the Church was consacrated by Pope Eugene IV. The lantern of the cupola was added in 1461, and the façade was built as late as 1887 by the architect Emilio De Fabris.

The majestic building is certainly one of the most significant and carliest examples of Tuscan Gothic, elegant and restrained in its architectural ensemble, and admirable for the refined decoration in coloured marbles.

The Duomo *or* Cathedral — *Detail of the façade with its three large bronze doors.* ➤
Above the central door there is a marble relief representing the Madonna in Glory, motif which inspired the decoration of the façade.

THE INTERIOR — The church is in the form of a latin cross with three naves separated by great pilasters and a choir from which extend the two lateral transepts and the semi-circular apse. The austere appearance and extreme simplicity enhance the vastness of the ambience. Considering the length — 150 meters or c. 450 feet — this church is the 3rd largest of the Christian world after St. Peter's in Rome and St. Paul's in London.

Fundamentally following the gothic style, the massive cathedral maintains, however, a kind of moderation and a classical feeling that Florence had inherited directly from Rome.

The sharp contrasts and vertical reach characteristic of the gothic are here restrained in the search for a composure that is based on the perfect square. The height of the central nave and the width of the church are each 38 meters in measure.

A place of many ceremonies and the memorable preachings of the Dominican monk Savonarola, the Cathedral was also the stage for the terrible assault called the "Pazzi Conspiracy". On Easter Sunday of 1478 assassins commissioned by Pope Sixtus IV and the Pazzi family tried to murder Lorenzo il Magnifico and his brother Giuliano of the Medici family. In the conspiracy, Giuliano was killed while his brother Lorenzo, with the help of friends, was able to save himself hiding in one of the sacresties of the church.

In addition, the Interior of the Basilica ccontains interesting works of art by Paolo Uccello, Andrea del Castagno, and Domenico di Michelino.

Paolo Uccello:
equestrian
monument
of John
Hawkwood
(1436).

Andrea del
Castagno:
equestrian
monument of
Niccolò da
Tolentino
(1456).

Interior — Famous
fresco by Domenico
di Michelino re-
presenting Dante
(right) enlightening
Florence with the Di-
vine Comedy. To the
left, Hell; in the bak-
ground, Purgatory;
above, Paradise.

Duomo *or* Cathedral — *Crypt of Santa Reparata: Following recent excavations the remains of the ancient Basilica of Santa Reparata, on which the actual Cathedral was built, were brought to light. During the restoration it was faithfully reconstructed according to the old basilical plan divided into three naves. The most important findings are some monumental slabs and a fresco representing the Resurrection, attributed to Giotto's school.*

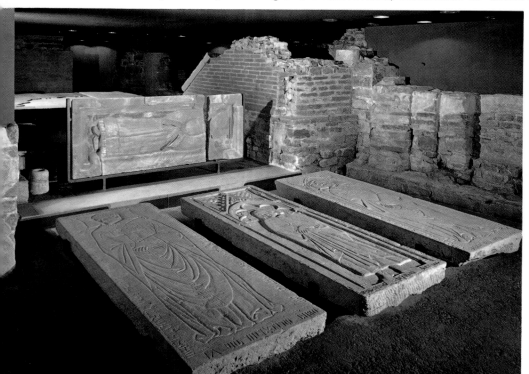

Apse and Cu- ➤
pola by Brunel-
leschi.

Cathedrale - Crypt of Santa Reparata — *Detail of the Resurrection: figures of the Madonna, shown at the left of Christ. The photo at the top right shows a view of the crypt. Group of stone monumental slabs.*

Duomo or Cathedral (St. Mary of the Flower) — Panoramic view, in which the grandiose unwinding of the construction is evident, from the rythmical sides to the agitated grouping of the radiating domed chapels; above rises the colossal dome placed on the imposing octagonal drum and divided into sections by the massive white ribs that culminate in the marble lantern; height approx. 350 ft. In this famous monument, architectural elements of various styles merge together, admirably unified by the green, white and pink marble which covers the entire exterior of the Cathedral.

GIOTTO'S CAMPANILE — The Campanile, 82 metres high, is considered one of the most beautiful in the world. Florentine Gothic in style, it is completely faced with marble in several colours and warm tones. The work was conceived and begun by Giotto in 1334. On this death (1337), the work was continued by Andrea Pisano and subsequently by Francesco Talenti, who faithfully followed Giotto's design with its beautiful two-mullioned windows and the most elegant three-mullioned window of the highest part. The lower band of the Campanile has a series of panels carved by great artists, such as Andrea Pisano and Luca della Robbia; they depict the story of the progressive civilising of man.
The delicate decoration with coloured marble merges admirably with the rest of the building, thus giving it a marvellous unity of style and colouring.

THE BAPTISTERY, or Basilica of St. John the Baptist — This was the ancient Cathedral of Florence before Santa Maria del Fiore was built. The building, in Romanesque style, dates from the 11th century. A geometric division of space is outlined on the exterior by coloured marbles, wich stress the architectural features of the building.

Three gilt bronze doors correspond to the cardinal points (the East Door, the North Door, and the South Door), ennobling the lines of the Baptistery.

« Il mio bel San Giovanni », as Dante was wont to call it, became the Baptistery of Florence in 1128.

THE BAPTISTRY — Eastern side with the Gates of Paradise, masterpiece by Lorenzo Ghiberti. Above the architrave is a statuary group by Andrea Sansovino representing Christ and St. John the Baptist, with an Angel by Innocenzo Spinazzi.

THE BAPTISTERY - Interior — An octagonal structure above an order of Corinthian columns. The decoration with marble in two colours, wich follows and emphasizes the geometrical division of the volumes, is repeated in the interior also. In the upper part, along the walls, runs a gallery of mullioned windows (Women's gallery). Also noteworthy are the inlaid pavement and the cupola, completely covered with mosaic. Along the walls of the Baptistery are placed some remarkable works, such as Donatello's celebrated Mary Magdalene, the same artist's St. John the Baptist, and the Tomb of the Antipope John XXII.

Dante, as he himself mentions was baptized at the font which formerly stood in this Church.

THE BAPTISTERY - Interior — Byzantine mosaics of the cupola (14th century). Note in the fore-ground the large figure of Christ the Universal Judge, often attributed to Cimabue, and in the centre part of the cupola, the representations in the Byzantine manner of the generations of the Angels.

THE BAPTISTRY — To the left are shown the South Doors, work of Andrea Pisano; to the right the North Doors, done by Ghiberti following the famous contest of 1401. Both doors are subdivided into 28 panels in which biblical stories are admirably shown in relief.

THE BAPTISTRY — *The East Door, the Gate of Paradise as it was called by Michelangelo, who admired its marvellous execution and originality as compared with the other two. It is the masterpiece of Lorenzo Ghiberti, who worked on it for 27 years, from 1425 to 1452. The Gate has 10 panels in gilt bronze, showing stories from the Old Testament. The subjects are treated concisely and clearly; the style represents an interesting departure from the art of the period; the transition from, and in part the abandonment of, Gothic linearism in favour of a clearer spatial arrangement of the volumes, and the adoption of perspective, heralding the Renaissance.*

LOGGIA DEL BIGALLO — *In front of the Southern doors, on the corner of Via Calzaiuoli, is the Loggia del Bigallo, built in late Gothic style by Alberto Arnoldi between 1352-1358 for the Compagnia della Misericordia, who would display the abandoned babies for adoption.*

The Creation of Adam and Eve; original sin; the expulsion from the Garden of Eden.
◄

The first human labours, Abel the shepherd and Cain ploughing the fields; slaying of Abel; God rebukes Cain.
►

Stories of Noah: the end of the Deluge; the drunkenness of Noah. In the background Mount Ararat.
◄

Abraham and Isaac: Angel appearing to Abraham; sacrifice of Isaac; Angel stops hand of Abraham.
►

◄
Jacob and Esau: Birth of Jacob and Esau; the sale of the primogeniture; Isaac orders Esau to the hunt; Rebecca advises Jacob; the deception of Isaac.

Stories of Joseph: Joseph sold to the merchants and brought to the Pharaoh; Joseph interpreting the Pharaoh's dream; discovery of the golden cup in Benjamin's dream; Jospeh recognized by his brothers.
►

Stories of Moses: Moses receives the tables of the Law on Mt. Sinai; the Israelites awaiting the return of Moses at the foot of the Mountain.

◄

Stories of Joshua: Joshua crossing the Jordan with the people of Israel; the battle of Jericho.

►

David and Goliath: battle with the Philistines; David kills Goliath; David with the head of Goliath.

◄

King Solomon receiving the Queen of Sheba in the temple.

►

In the richly decorated frame around the panels are 24 niches containing magnificent statuettes of Prophets, Sibyls and other biblical characters, alternated with roundels from which protrude heads that, for the most part, are portraits of artists that were contemporaries of Ghiberti. Photo on the left: self portrait of the artist and of his step-father. Bartoluccio.
On the right, figures of the Prophets Isaiah and Johua.

Museum of the Opera del Duomo

MUSEUM OF THE OPERA DEL DUOMO — Directly behind the apse of the Cathedral, at n. 9, is situated the Museum of the Opera del Duomo, that contains works of art taken from the Baptistry, Cathedral and Campanile and also remains of architecture pre-existent to these constructions. Crossing the vestibule and other small rooms in which crests, architectural fragments and various works are conserved, one comes to the large room in which statues are gathered that adorned the old façade of the Cathedral, demolished in 1587; of notable interest are the four statues of the Evangelists that were originally in the niches around the central door. In small adjoining rooms precious minor art objects are displayed: reliquaries, miniatured missals, enamelled works, altar frontals, vestments. Climbing the steps one comes to the large room of the Cantorias in which are two magnificent choir lofts sculpted in marble and taken from the Cathedral in 1686: on the left, work by Luca della Robbia, with ten high reliefs set between pilasters in which the artist portrayed elegant and joyous figures of children singing and dancing; directly opposite, the choir loft by Donatello consisting of a single relief of lively dancing children. In the same room are other statues by Donatello representing prophets that were originally located in the niches of the Bell-tower. Finally one passes to the room in which numerous projects and models for the drum of the cupola, the lantern and the façade are displayed.

DONATELLO — *Choir Loft (Cantoria): unusual work penetrated by a dynamic plastic sense, which reflects the classical inspiration of the artist evident after his Roman sojourn of* 1431.

LUCA DELLA ROBBIA — *Choir Loft: Detail of one panel: This work was done in* 1439. ➤

23

The Pietà

One of the most important pieces of sculpture preserved in the Cathedral Museum is the "Pietà", a master-piece by Michelangelo Buonarroti and sculpted towards the end of his life. Michelangelo was almost eighty years old when for the third time he chose the subject of the deposition. This "Pietà" was to be a part of his tomb and the artist sculpted his self-portrait in the hooded figure of Nicodemus. On the right is the Virgin whose face is almost disfigured in the suffering; in the middle Christ's body yields completely in death and is only with great effort supported by His Mother and Nicodemus. On the left is Mary Magdalen, which was sculpted later by Tiberio Calcagni. Michelangelo, dissatisfied with the quality of the marble, tried to destroy the work and left it unfinished.

ORSANMICHELE — Walking along Via Calzaiuoli one reaches the imposing and magnificent church of Orsanmichele. Built by Francesco Talenti, Neri Fioravante and Benci di Cione it was originally an open loggia used as a grain market; later Simone Talenti closed the arches with elegant International Gothic decoration and added the two upper stories. All around the exterior of the building one can admire the niches containing statues of the patron saints of the guilds; the interior, divided in two naves by large pillars, is frescoed with images of the Saints not represented on the outside. In the back, the beautiful marble tabernacle by Andrea Orcagna, a masterpiece of Gothic sculpture.

PIAZZA DELLA SIGNORIA — This was, and still is today, the political centre of Florence. Here stands the marvellous Palazzo della Signoria, or Palazzo Vecchio, which rises majestically with its bold Torre dei Foraboschi, some 94 metres high. Next to it is the Fountain of Neptune, with the famous « Biancone », a not very successful work by Ammannati, and the bronze statues of marine deities. Beside the fountain stands the equestrian monument to Cosimo I of the Medici, by Giambologna. At the other side of the Palazzo Vecchio is the Loggia della Signoria.
The Piazza della Signoria is undoubtedly one of the most beautiful squares in the world, both on account of the famous works of art gathered there, and for the impressive harmony of the whole.

LOGGIA OF THE SIGNORIA — Also called of Orcagna or of the Lanzi (Lancers): Under the wide arches or this elegant, Florentine-Gothic construction, numerous statues are gathered, including some famous masterpieces: Left photo, the Rape of Polyxena, one of the most beautiful 19th cent. Florentine sculptures, by Pio Fedi; centre, Menelaus supporting the body of Patroclus, copy of an original Greek statue of the 4th cent. B.C.; right, Hercules fighting the Centaur Nessus by Giambologna.

PIAZZA DELLA SIGNORIA — Also in front of the Palazzo Vecchio there are well known works of sculpture: in the foreground, Hercules and Cacus, by Baccio Bandinelli; next a copy of Michelangelo's famous David; behind, the dramatic bronze group of Judith and Holofernes, one of the last works by Donatello. Left, detail of the monumental Fountain of Neptune by Ammannati.

LOGGIA DELLA SIGNORIA - Perseus, by Benvenuto Cellini — *A bronze statue executed by him in 1553. This sculpture of the great Florentine goldsmith is the final version of a previous small wax model, considered by all the critics to be more beautiful and poetic owing to the greater simplicity and compactness of the body of Perseus.*

LOGGIA DEI PRIORI, or DELLA SIGNORIA — It stands in Piazza della Signoria, with its three fine, wide arches. It was built between 1367 and 1382 to the design of Benci di Cione and Simone Talenti. It shows a marvellous fusion of Gothic art, now at its last stage, and the art of the Renaissance. The Loggia was used for public meetings and ceremonies.

28

Today it contains ancient Roman sculptures and the work of 14th century artists. Among these we would mention: Perseus (Cellini); the Rape of the Sabine Women (Giambologna); Menelaus supporting Patroclus (copy of an ancient Greek sculpture); the Rape of Polyxena (Fedi); Hercules and the Centaur (Giambologna); and others.

LOGGIA DELLA SIGNORIA — *The Rape of the Sabine Women, an interestint group executed by Giambologna in 1583. We are struck by the dynamic force of the composition and the spiral arrangement of the group, which thus seems to conquer the space around it and make it revolve with the whole group.*

Palazzo Vecchio

PALAZZO VECCHIO — Also called Palazzo della Signoria or Palazzo del Popolo, consists of the front section facing the Square, built between 1298-1314 probably designed by Arnolfo di Cambio, and various additions built in later years. The principal building, a massive construction covered with characteristic ashlar, is lightened by the elegant mullioned windows inserted in robust round arches and by the thrust of the tower built on the site of the pre-existing tower of the « Foraboschi ». The three stories of the Palace are divided by thin cornices and surmounted by an imposing projecting crenellated gallery, motif repeated in the tower. The Palazzo Vecchio, superb example of Florentine civic architecture, for a time also served as a home to the Medici family until Cosimo I moved to the Pitti Palace.

PALAZZO VECCHIO - Interior — Courtyard by Michelozzo (1453). The original Renaissance Architecture of this courtyard has been somewath spoiled by Baroque decorations, which, while enriching the surfaces, make the whole rather heavy.
In the centre of the couryard, on a porphyry basin (by Battista Tadda), is the vinged Putto with a fish, a fine work by Andrea del Verrocchio (1476). It has recently been replaced by a copy. According to the original plan of Michelangelo and the Government of Florence, the statue of David was tho have been placed in this courtyard.

PALAZZO VECCHIO

Interior — The elegant marble portal of the Sala dei Gigli (Room of the Lilies), surmounted by the delicate statue of St. John the Baptist and four putti with festoons by Benedetto da Maiano.

The viverly bronze statue of a boy with a dolphin, masterpiece by Verrocchio.

The Studiolo of Francesco I, elegant room with barrel vaulted ceiling created by Vasari.

The Battle of San Vincenzo a Mare near Populonia, won by the Florentines. (Vasari.)

PALAZZO VECCHIO - Interior – Salone dei cinquecento: On the other page three of the large frescoes that decorate the walls of this vast room are shown. Top: « The Conquest of Siena », Bottom left: « The Conquest of Porto Ercole » and Bottom right: « The Emperor Maximilian during the siege of Leghorn », all works by Giorgio Vasari.

The Battle of Marciano in Val di Chiana.

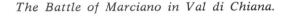

PALAZZO VECCHIO - Interior — « Salone dei Cinquecento ». It was built in 1495 to a design by Cronaca for the meetings of the General Council of the People. This is one of the largest public assembly halls in existence. The walls, which are now decorated with frescoes by Vasari showing battle scenes of Cosimo I, had originally to be

PALAZZO VECCHIO - Interior — Hercules and Diomedes (Vincenzo de Rossi). This sculpture is found, together with many others, in the « Salons dei Cinquecento », and forms part of the cycle of the Labours of Hercules, executed by the same artist.

adorned with frescoes by the two greatest artists of the 16th century, Michelangelo and Leonardo da Vinci; these works were never executed. The walls of the Hall are adorned with precious tapestries and various sculptures. On the ceiling is a serie of frescoes extolling the City of Florence and its illustrious rulers, the Medici.

PALAZZO VECCHIO - Interior - The Victory — *by Michelangelo Buonarroti - 1525. This was done for Julius's Tomb.*

UFFIZI GALLERY — From the Piazzale degli Uffizi, next to the Piazza della Signoria, one comes to the famous Uffizi Gallery which contains one of the richest collections of art treasures in the world. In it are included the most significant works and numerous masterpieces of the Italian schools of art, in particular the Florentine school, and an important group of Flemmish paintings. The Gallery came about through the initiative of the Grand Duke Francesco I who wanted to gather his first artistic collections together in one place. Originally the museum was limited to the famous Tribune, purposely built by Buontalenti, and to the first corridor. Since then it has been continuously enlarged, first by the Medici and later by the Dukes of Lorraine. It was finally organized by Grand Duke Cosimo III and was considerably enriched by the inheritance of Cardinal Leopoldo de' Medici. Anna Maria Ludovica, the last Medici, willed to the Tuscan State the immense patrimony that included paintings, sculptures, bronzes, an enormous quantity of artistic furnishings, important archeological collections and collections of scientific equipment and arms. The Gallery has been reorganized at various times: between 1780-1782 the original entrance was replaced by the present one facing the Piazzale degli Uffizi; between 1830-1865 the archeological collections and the numerous Romanesque, Gothic and Renaissance sculptures were transported elsewhere. During the last war the works of art were removed from the gallery and after, the collections were again reorganized and many of the rooms remodelled.

PIAZZALE DEGLI UFFIZI — *Under the beautiful portico that borders the Piazzale degli Uffizi are many stalls that sell characteristic Florentine handicrafts, leather items, small reproductions of statues and paintings, and a wide variety of painted wooden articles.*

UFFIZI-GALLERY - Corridor III - *This is one of the two long corridors in the Gallery wich are joined by a smaller one. Along their walls are placed Greek and Roman sculptures, both originals and copies, together with most valuable tapestries from the best workshops.*

◄ ►

SANDRO BOTTI-CELLI — *Artist with an exquisitely delicate style and refined taste. In his compositions, animated by a melancholy and musical rhythm, relive the classical myths of Spring, Venus, Zephyr and Flora. In the photo to the side and on the right, « The Birth of Venus »; below « La Primavera » (Springtime).*

BOTTICELLI — *Annunciation.*

BACCHUS — *Young work by Michelangelo Merisi called Il Caravaggio, which already reveals the genius of this artist who revolutionized 16th cent. Italian painting and brought art back to a vivid sense of reality.*

TITIAN — *Venus with Little Dog (1538), also known as Venus of Urbino: admirable for the delicacy and chiaroscuro of the beautiful nude and for the warm luminosity that permeates the entire painting.*

LEONARDO DA VINCI — *Annunciation: young work of the artist.*

Portraits of Federigo da Montefeltro and his wife Battista Sforza, painted in 1466 by Piero della Francesca.

UFFIZI GALLERY — *Filippo Lippi (1406-1469): Madonna and Child. This sensitive composition, painted in 1465, is rightly considered Lippi's masterpiece. A calm, pensive serenity and a sweetness of attitude and expression blend marvellously the figures of the Madonna, Child and the infant St. John, giving the picture its lyrical harmony.*

UFFIZI GALLERY — *Holy family: Michelangelo Buonarroti (1475-1564). This is the first of his paintings that has come down to us. The group has been conceived like a sculptor's single block of stone, where the masses are intertwined in a spiral and are grouped in lively contrast. The beautiful nude figures in the background are warmer in tone, while the semi-circle of the wall opens upon a more generalized prospect.*

Top left: detail of the Madonna of the Cold-finch, painted by RA-PHAEL in 1506 for the wedding of his friend Lorenzo Nasi. The sweet face is animated by a warm light that gives life to the color and brightens the soft chiaroscuro. Top right: Flora, one of Titian's most famous works, in which the artist represents his ideal type of feminine beauty. To the side: the Baccante by Annibale Carracci.

To the side - two of the portraits of the Medici family exhibited in the Tribune: Top - Cosimo the Elder by Pontormo; *Below - Lorenzo the Magnificent by Vasari. Above - Eve - painting by Luca Cranach the Elder.*

PITTI PALACE — In rivalry with the richest families of the city, Luca Pitti, jealous and powerful Florentine banker who contended the supremecy of the Medici, commissioned Filippo Brunelleschi in 1440 to design the most grandiose and monumental palace in Florence. The original project, of purely classical inspiration, was to consist of a ground floor with three portals and two upper stories with seven windows, each inserted in large arches. Following a conspiracy against the leaders of the city, the Pitti family went bankrupt and the palace was later bought by Eleanor di Toledo, wife of Grand Duke Cosimo I. The construction was amplified at various times; first by Bartolomeo Ammannati who opened two enormous windows on the ground floor and built the magnificent courtyard which is one of the most beautiful and important works of 16th cent architecture, in that, for the first time, a courtyard and palace open directly on to the gardens, thus realizing a perfect fusion between architecture and nature. The palace attained its actual dimensions following additions by various 17th and 18th century artists. Today the Pitti Palace is the home of extremely important Museums and Galleries including the famous Palatine Gallery, the Royal Appartments, the Gallery of Modern Art, the Treasure Room (Museo degli Argenti) and the Museum of Antique Coaches.

BOBOLI GARDENS — *Above: view of the 17th century amphitheatre and, in the foreground, the Fountain of the Artichoke by* Francesco del Tadda. *Below: the Ocean Fountain by* Giambologna, *one of the most beautiful creations of its kind, surrounded by symbolic statues of 3 rivers; Nile, Ganges and Euphrates. In the water: 2 islands with Perseus and Andromeda.*

In the famous PALATINE GALLERY are gathered numerous masterpieces of the Italian (with particular emphasis on Titian and Raphael), Spanish and Flemmish schools. The large collection was begun by Grand Duke Cosimo II in 1620 and continuously enriched by the Medici family and later by the Lorraines. The paintings are not set up following specific chronological and artistical criteria, but rather with purely decorative intentions, according to the taste of the 17th century. In the photo: the first room of the Gallery called the room of the ILIAD because of the frescoes on the ceiling and in the lunettes by Luigi Sabatelli, that were inspired by the famous Homeric poem.

Top left: ANNUNCIA-
TION by Andrea del
Sarto.

To the side: MADONNA
AND CHILD — famous
work by Murillo.

Below: THE CONSE-
QUENCES OF WAR by
Peter Paul Rubens.

ROOM OF SATURN — Gets its name from the frescoes on the ceiling, painted by Ciro Ferri on designs by Pietro da Cortona, that exalt the virtues and merits of the Medici Dynasty through the use of mythological representations. In this room, the second of the Gallery, are works by Raphael, Andrea del Sarto, Perugino and others.

PALAZZO PITTI - Palatine Gallery — The Madonna of the Chair, a famous and much admired picture by Raphael, painted in 1515. The pictorial conception of this Madonna, who in type is a woman of the people, is original, and above all, touchingly intimate, as she sits on a chair, lovingly clasping her little son to her breast.

Two other famous works by RAPHAEL: The Madonna dell'Impannata, so called because the figures are shown in a room whose window is covered with a linen panel, was sketched by the master in 1514 but probably painted by his followers. La Velata (The Veiled Woman) - probably a portrait of La Fornarina (baker's daughter), is one of the masterpieces of the Italian Renaissance.

RAPHAEL — *Portrait of Cardinal Bernardo Dovizi da Bibbiena.*

RAPHAEL — *Madonna of the Grand Duke.*

JUSTUS SUSTERMANS — *Portrait of Prince Waldemar Christian of Denmark.*

GODFRIED SCHALKEN — *Girl with a Candle.*

FORMER ROYAL APPARTMENTS — *Above: the luxurious Throne Room adorned with tapestries and portraits of the Medici painted by Sustermans. Below: Room of the Niches (Dining Room) so called because of the niches containing copies of classical statues; here also is a collection of Medici portraits by Sustermans and, on the furniture, original Sèvres and antique Japanese vases.*

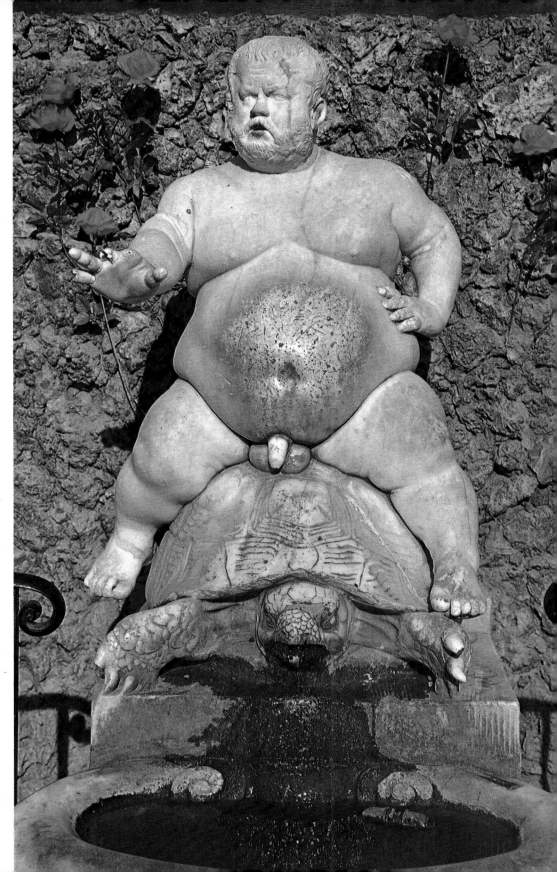

PALAZZO PITTI — *Boboli Gardens. The « Bacchino » (the little Bacchus- is a portrait of Pietro Barbino, court jester of Cosimo I, who became the symbol of the care-free Florence of the people. The statue, mistakenly believed to be a small drunken Bacchus, represents the tiny, plump, almost obese dwarf, whose task it was to amuse the gentlefolk of the period.*

PETER PAUL RU-BENS — *The Four Philosophers (Palatine Gallery): The artist (standing) portrays himself and his brother Philip conversing with the distinguished philologist and philosopher Justus Lipsius and Jan Van der Wouver, pupil together with Philip of Lipsius; in the niche a bust of Seneca.*

The extremely simple yet characteristic façade of the Church of Santo Spirito certainly does not suggest the beauty of the interior, in the form of a Latin cross with 3 naves. In this last work by Brunelleschi, begun in 1444 and finished by his followers, the great art of this master reaches its climax: 40 semi-circular chapels that radiate around the entire perimeter, an abundance of columns with Corinthian capitals and the play of arches and vaults, animate the space, giving life to uniquely harmonious perspectives.

Various views of the popular section of San Frediano: the massive Porta Romana, that opens on the only remaining piece of the old fortifications of the city; the Church of San Frediano in Cestello and, on the right, the Porta San Frediano, built in 1324 following a project by Andrea Pisano. The Gate, that still conserves the massive, antique doors, is situated at the beginning of Via Pisana.

PONTE VECCHIO – Not only is this the oldest bridge of the city, but also one of the most famous bridges in the world. It already existed in the 10th century, but was destroyed by the Arno in the flood in 1333. After it had been rebuilt in stone about the middle of the 14 th century by Neri di Fioravante, it was reserved, by order of FerdinandI, exclusively for goldsmiths. In fact, these set up their shops here and built their little houses at the back of them, projecting over the Arno. The effect of this is unique and most picturesque, so that the bridge is a « must » for every tourist. Under one of the arches of the bridge, which breaks the row of shops, a bust of Benvenuto Cellini, the greatest Florentine goldsmith, has been placed. Along the upper part of the bridge runs Vasari's famous passageway.

Church of Santa Maria del Carmine

CHURCH OF SANTA MARIA DEL CARMINE — Begun in 1268 in Romanesque-Gothic style, it was enlarged and remodelled many times in successive eras. It was reconstructed in 1771 after a fire destroyed a major part of the complex, saving only the Corsini and Brancacci Chapels. The 18th cent. interior is in the form of a Latin cross with one nave. Of exceptional interest is the Brancacci Chapel, situated at the end of the right trancept. Commissioned by Felice Brancacci, rich merchant and political figure, enemy of the Medici, it contains a cycle of frescoes that are among the most significant and revolutionary works of Italian art which appeared at the start of the Renaissance. The artists involved are Masolino da Panicale and his pupil Massaccio, the great innovator of the 15th century that here created his masterpiece, and later Filippino Lippi. The various stories, subdivided into scenes, are organized according to rigorous perspective rules, true realization of space in which the figures of Christ, the Saints and Angels shed all residual of mysticism and become of a serious and pensive humanity.

MASOLINO — *St. Peter resuscitates Tabitha.*   MASACCIO — *St. Peter Distributing Alms.*

In the first fresco on the top left is the EXPULSION FROM PARADISE, masterpiece by Massaccio. The scene has tremendous dramatic power obtained through the clean-cut plasticity and bold chiaroscuro of the forms. The figures are caught in a moment of intense expression: Eve who has already acquired a sense of modesty, shouts her desperation and Adam, more contained, covers his face with his hands.

Founded, according to legend, by Charlemagne, the CHURCH OF SANTI APOSTOLI
in reality dates back to the end of the 11th cent. Although it underwent various tran-
sformations and was recently restored, the church still conserves some original architecture. The interior, which has been brought back to its original basilical aspect, is
divided into three naves. In this church some stone chips are preserved which legend
says were brought from Jerusalem by Pazzino dei Pazzi returning from the first Cru-
sade. On Holy Saturday they are used to light the sacred fire which is solemnly taken
to the Baptistry of St. John the Baptist.

LOGGIA DEL MERCATO NUOVO — *The Bronze Boar, known as the « Porcellino » (little pig), made by Pietro Tacca in 1612. The Loggia, with its series of round arches, is a typical example of Renaissance architecture. It was designed by Giovanni del Tasso, who built it between 1547 and 1551. In the Loggia, characteristic products of Florentine artisans are sold. In the pavement, a round slab marks the spot where, in the 16th century, merchants guilty of fraudulent bankruptcy, were exposed to public scorn. The Loggia is commonly called the « Straw Market ».*

In Piazza Santa Trinita rises the most grandiose medieval Florentine palace, the **SPINI-FERRONI PALACE**, built in 1289, with 3 stories of windows and an imposing projecting battlement.

CHURCH OF THE HOLY TRINITY — *Built in the 11th century for the monks of Vallombrosa, and enlarged in the 13th and 14th centuries. The façade was built towards the end of the 16th century by Bernardo Buontalenti. In the interior there are interesting works of art by Luca della Robbia, Desiderio da Settignano, Lorenzo Monaco and Ghirlandaio. In one of the chapels is the large Crucifix of San Giovanni Gualberto, which, according to the legend, bowed its head before the Saint adoring it. Beside the Church of the Holy Trinity is the 13th century Palazzo Gianfigliazzi, and opposite, the magnificent Palazzo Merlato Spini-Ferroni.*

HOLY TRINITY BRIDGE — After having been destroyed several times by the river in flood, it was rebuilt by Bartolomeo Ammannati between 1557 and 1569, under Michelangelo's artistic influence. It was again destroyed during the Second World War (1944). It has recently been rebuilt in accordance with Ammannati's design, using the same material which had fallen into the Arno. The four statues at the entrance of the bridge are of the 17th century. It is one of the most significant examples of Renaissance architecture, since it combines elegance of line with the functional solidity of its masonry.

SUNSETS AND NOCTURNAL SCENES OF FLORENCE — A beautiful sunset behind the Holy Trinity Bridge, a

view of the Ponte Vecchio illuminated during the feast of St. John and two nocturnal scenes of the Lungarni.

A characteristic view of ARNOLFO'S TOWER, which rises imposingly and daringly above the Palazzo della Signoria, seen from Via dei Neri.

The beautiful hexagonal bell-tower of the BADIA FIORENTINA, Benedictine church founded in 978, seen from the elegant Renaissance cloister. ➤

The austere DAVANZATI PA-
LACE, most distinguished example
of a typical 14th cent. Florentine
private palace; the loggia was added in the 15th cent. All around
this palace are the old tower-hous-
es, strongholds of the most powerful Florentine families and testimony of the bitter internal
fighting that took place in the
city.

In the photo to the side, the Baroque façade of the CHURCH OF OGNISSANTI built in 1251 and completely remodelled in the 17th century. Next to it rises the beautiful Romanesque campanile. Below left; the PALAZZO DI PARTE GUELFA, built in the 14th cent. and amplified in the following century by Filippo Brunelleschi. Below right; the ANTINORI PALACE of noble simplicity with its façade of smooth ashlar divided by elegant cornices.

Right, the STROZZI PALACE (seen at night in the photo below). Considered the most beautiful palace of the Florentine Renaissance, it is testimony to the splendour of Florence during that era. Begun by Benedetto da Maiano and continued by Cronaca, it consists of 3 stories entirely covered with slightly graded rough stone blocks and is crowned with Cronaca's elegante wide cornice.

Below, another masterpiece of Renaissance architecture: the RUCELLAI PALACE, designed by Leon Battista Alberti, with its admirable rhythm of 3 orders of slightly projecting pilasters which support elaborate trabeations. On the top floors are elegant mullioned windows inserted in round arches.

The beautiful façade of the CHURCH OF SANTA MARIA NOVELLA, begun by the Dominican Friars Sisto and Ristoro and completed by Jacopo Talenti, is in Romanesque-Gothic style and characterized by the two-tone marble decoration and the geometrical division of space typical of Florentine architecture. The upper part, designed by Leon Battista Alberti, is Renaissance and offers an original innovation in the 2 volutes that connect the lateral and central parts together gracefully.

Interior (right) is in the form of a « T » with 3 naves separated by pillars that support acute arches and cross vaults. Looking towards the altar the pillars are placed slightly closer together thus creating the illusion of more profound depth.

Across the square directly opposite to the church is the LOGGIA OF ST. PAUL, inspired by Brunelleschi's portico of the Foundling Hospital. The glazed terracotta medallions are by Giovanni della Robbia.

The vault and walls of the Chancel of Santa Maria Novella were frescoed by DOMENICO GHIRLANDAIO and helpers, among whom was young Michelangelo. Pictured, The Birth of the Madonna. To the side, The triumph of Saint Thomas Aquinas, fresco by Andrea di Bonaiuto that is found in the SPANISH CHAPEL, old chapter room later taken over by the Grand Duchess Eleanor of Toledo and used for religious functions by her Spanish following.

Basilica of San Lorenzo

In Piazza San Lorenzo rises the unfinished façade of the ancient Basilica of
SAN LORENZO, consecrated in 393, renovated in Romanesque style in the
11th cent. and again transformed by Brunelleschi on commission of the
Medici. Of particular interest is the picturesque complex made up of the
loggia that covers the cupola of the main chapel, the large 17th cent. dome
of the Chapel of the Princes, the slim campanile and Michelangelo's low
cupola of the New Sacristy with its elegant lantern.

A view of the CLOISTER OF SAN LORENZO, with the bottom arches resting on Ionic columns supporting a loggia with slimmer columns. In the background, the cupola of the Chapel of the Princes. In the side photo, a view of the picturesque market that animates San Lorenzo Square.

The interior of the Church of San Lorenzo repeats the plan of the Paleochristian basilica with 3 naves, trancept and panelled ceiling. Brunelleschi has made this church one of the most beautiful examples of Florentine Renaissance architecture, with its clear division of space, and exact and harmonious correspondence of all the parts emphasized by the rational use of the white plaster and grey stone.

CHURCH OF SAN LORENZO - Chapel of the Princes — This sumptuous and majestic ➤ chapel was intended by the Medici family as their personal chapel. It was begun in 1604 by Matteo Nigetti, who improved on a design by Giovanni dei Medici. It has an octagonal plan, culminating in a very slender cupola. The walls and floor are completely covered with precious marbles and other hard stones. At the sides, the monumental sarcophagi of the Grand-Dukes. The two statues of gilt bronze are by Tacca. On the lower band of the walls are depicted 16 coats of arms of cities belonging to the Grand Duchy of the Medici.

General view of the NEW SACRISTY, first actual architectural realization by Michelangelo, that takes its inspiration from Brunelleschi's Old Sacristy. In contrast to Brunelleschi's clear, serene and logical division of space, Michelangelo's structure, although also clear and well defined, is animated by a more intense and dramatic sense of plasticity. The grey stone membering is bold and accentuated in order to emphasize all the other architectural elements that enliven the surface. In this beautiful setting, which merges sculpture and architecture, Michelangelo placed the tombs of the Medici dedicated to Giuliano Duke of Nemours, Lorenzo Duke of Urbino and Lorenzo the Magnificent. On the latter tomb is the MADONNA AND CHILD (detail on the right), which, in the unusual position and contrasting movements of the bodies, presents the search for a new equilibrium, as though the artist were trying to express a sentiment both human and tragic.

Madonna and Child New Sacristy ➤
S. Lorenzo, Florence

TOMB OF GIULIANO DUKE OF NE-MOURS — *The tomb was conceived and realized by Michelangelo as a sarcophagus, with the statue of the Duke, idealized in the young figure of an ancient warrior, placed in a niche above. On the sarcophagus are the symbolic figures of Night, on whose face is seen a sense of profound melancholy, and Day, a powerful figure in whom the tragic twisting of the body is accompanied by the mysterious nonfinished face.*

◄

TOMB OF LORENZO DUKE OF UR-
BINO — *Conceived structurally like
that of Giuliano, this sarcophagus is
adorned with the beautiful figure of
Aurora (Dawn) whose harmonious,
stretching body follows the shape of
the volute and whose face betrays an
inner drama; and that of Dusk, a powerful and restless figure so conscious
of life's pain.*

➤

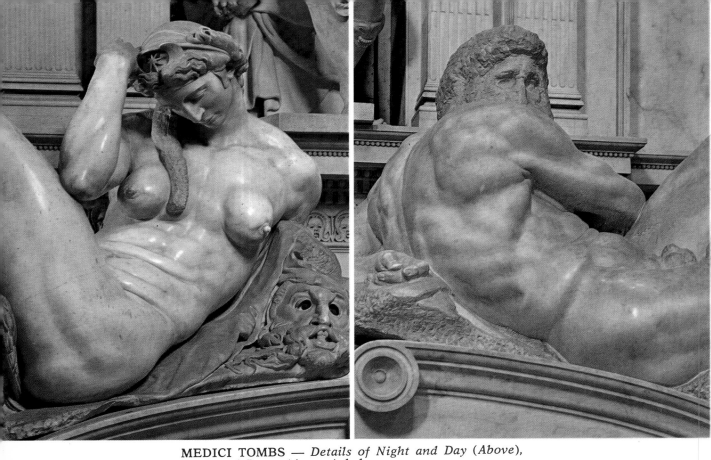

MEDICI TOMBS — *Details of Night and Day (Above), Dusk and Dawn (Aurora) below.*

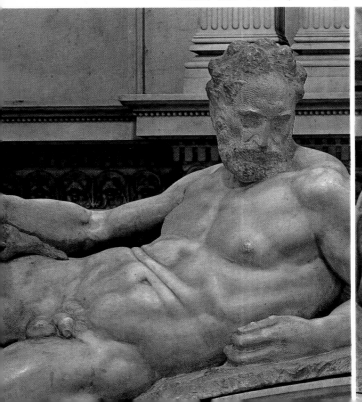

THE LAURENTIAN LIBRARY, besides containing valuable collections of rare books and manuscripts, is of extraordinary interest because of its architecture, one of Michelangelo's most ingenious creations. The building is made up of a complex and solemn vestibule, where the live and harmonious plasticity is centered in the original staircase, and a long rectangular room. Here Michelangelo's architectural concept finds amazing harmony and equilibrium that unify the tormented elements.

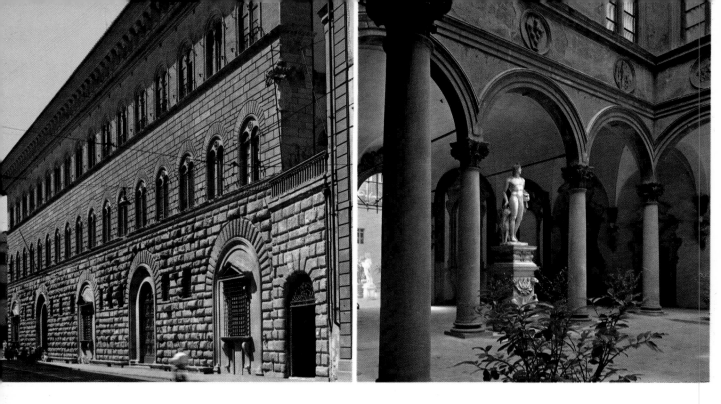

MEDICI-RICCARDI PALACE — *This magnificent example of a Florentine Renaissance palace, home of the Medici, was built by Michelozzo for Cosimo the Elder. Later it was considerably enlarged and finally became property of the Riccardi family. The beautiful façade, covered with various grades of ashlar, is enriched by a double series of elegant mullioned windows and culminates in the bold projecting cornice. Inside is a beautiful porticoed courtyard surmounted by a story of double arched windows and a loggia.*

In the Medici-Riccardi Palace is a Chapel built by Michelozzo and decorated with the famous fresco representing THE ADORATION OF THE MAGI by Benozzo Gozzoli. This simple and fresh representation gives great attention to the costumes of that era and reproduces portraits of the most well known persons of the times, from Lorenzo the Magnificent, to Pope Leo X to a self-portrait of the artist. On the side walls, Angels in Adoration are painted against an enchanting background (above photo).

The Church and Museum of St. Mark

THE CHURCH and CONVENT OF ST. MARK were built in the 13th century by the Sylvestrine monks and later restored and enlarged by Michelozzo. The actual façade was built in 1780 by G. Pronti in a simple Baroque style. Since 1869 the Convent houses a museum with works by Fra Angelico, creator of a serene art which is expressed in simple, clear compositions and in humble, delicate colours.

MUSEUM OF ST. MARK — *Fra Angelico (1387-1455). The Annunciation, a delicate composition which reveals the artist's spiritual serenity.*

THE FINAL JUDGEMENT, *masterpiece by Fra Angelico. Pictured below, details of the group of condemned on the right, and, on the left, the chosen as they join the angels in a joyous dance in the beautiful garden before the Gate of Paradise.*

FRA ANGELICO — *Madonna and Child with Saints.* ➤

FRA ANGELICO — *Crucifixion:* **At** *the foot of the 3 crosses besid-* **es** *the Madonna and St. John, numerous saints of religious orders are represented.* ⌄

Portrait of Fra Girolamo Savonarola by Fra Bartolomeo. ➤

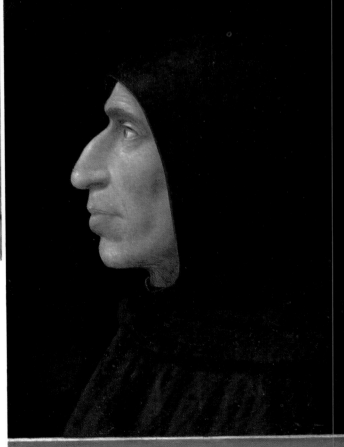

◄
*The central section of the TABERNACLE
OF THE LINAIUOLI, also by Angelico,
that represents the Madonna and Child
enthroned, placed in a setting of rich, gilt
drapery.*

HIERONYMI·FERRARIENSIS·ADE
ᴿ MISSI·PROPHETÆ·EFFIGIES·⊛

PIAZZA DELLA SANTISSIMA ANNUNZIATA — bordered on 3 sides by porticoes, offers an admirable example of Renaissance harmony, equilibrium and measure. On the left, the portico of the Confraternity of the Servites of Mary, work of Antonio da Sangallo and Baccio d'Agnolo; in the centre, the Church of the Santissima Annunziata, and right, the portico of the Hospital of the Innocents (Foundling Hospital). The Hospital, built as an orphanage, was begun in 1419 by Filippo Brunelleschi and is generally considered a revolutionary work which initiated a new era. For the first time architecture was presented with its division of space well defined and made in rapport to man.

THE PORTICO OF THE HOSPITAL OF THE INNOCENTS *consists of 9 elegant round arches resting on a flight of 9 steps and surmounted by a light architrave. The medallions above the arches are by Andrea della Robbia and represent swaddled children.*

THE CLOISTER OF THE HOSPITAL OF INNOCENTS, *with 5 arches per side, has recently been restored to its original aspect as conceived by Brunelleschi.*

Gallery of the Accademy

THE GALLERY OF THE ACCADEMY, formed in 1784 through the initiative of Grand Duke Pietro Leopoldo, contains, besides a notable collection of Florentine paintings, some of Michelangelo's most famous sculptures. In the large room, 4 of the Prisoners (also referred to as Slaves or Captives) originally destined for the tomb of Pope Julius II and, in the Tribune, built especially by Emilio De Fabris, is the famous DAVID.

DAVID - height 14ft. approx. — It was sculpted by Michelangelo in 1504 from ➤ a block of marble that had been begun then abandoned by another artist. The beautiful face of David showing pride in the determined cut of the profile and in the intent eyes; the nervous yet agile body; the magnificent hand holding the stone with its veins and nerves so well studied; all express the force, decision and nobility of the man and the strength and will of the hero.

A
THE PALESTRINA PIETA' — *extremely dramatic group.*

◄ THE SAINT MATTHEW – *Of the 12 Apostles that Michelangelo was commissioned to sculpt for the façade of the Cathedral of Florence, only this St. Matthew was begun.*

THE SYNAGOGUE — *Built in 1882 by the architects Falcini, Micheli and Treves, a picturesque Temple in the Oriental style.*

➤

Michelangelo's Home

In Michelangelo's home (CASA BUONARROTI), bought by him for his nephews and left to the city in 1858, young works of the artist are displayed. Below, THE BATTLE OF THE CENTAURS, marble relief dated around 1492, representing a tussle of nude forms, already shows signs of the future « unfinished » technique that becomes one the most important characteristics of Michelangelo's art.

Battle of the Centaurs
Casa Buonarroti, Florence

In the MADONNA OF THE STAIRS, so called because of the brief staircase on the left of the composition, the influence of Donatello is felt in the use of the « stiacciato » technique, but the signs of that expressive power and imposing form that become characteristics of the artist's maturity are already present.

◄ WOODEN CRUCIFIX, sculpted in 1494 for the Church of Santo Spirito, was recently found and identified with the help of some documents of the period that explain the method used to make this type of work.

Museum of the Bargello

THE PALACE OF THE BARGELLO was built in the middle of the 13th century as the seat of the Captain of the People; from 1261 it became the residence of the Podestà, called Bargello. The most suggestive part of the Palace is the courtyard which consists of an arcade under which ia a valuable collection of sculptures, and an open staircase leading to the balcony. The well in the centre indicates the site where executions took place, after having been announced by the dreaded tolling of the bell in the Tower called Volognana. Since 1865 the Palace has been the seat of the National Museum.

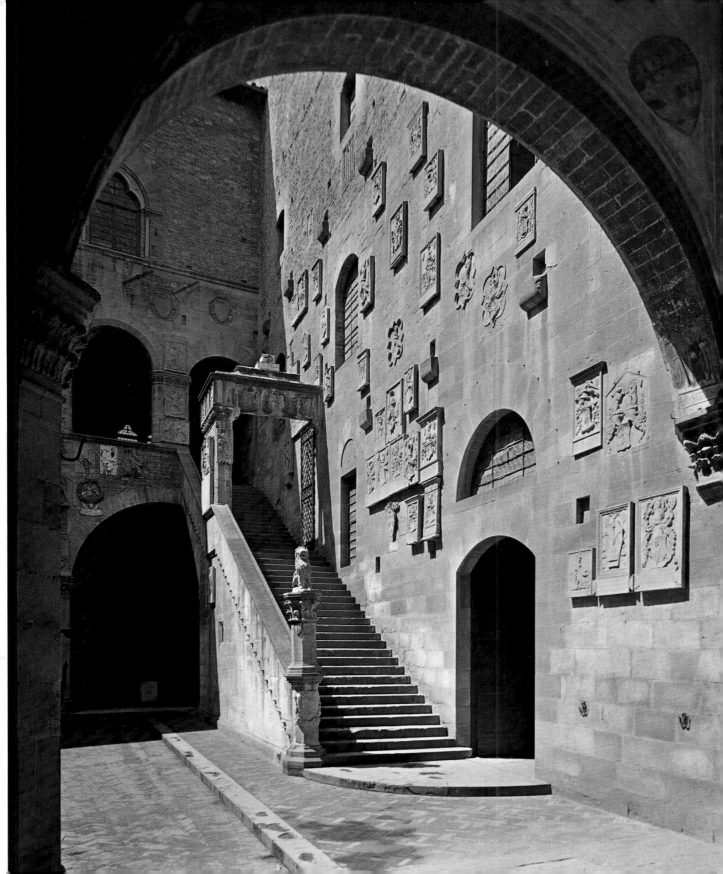

Under the arches of the balcony are displayed bronze works by Giambologna repre-senting an eagle, a gohawk, turkey and a peacock.

GIOVANNI DELLA ROBBIA — *Wreath with the insignias of the Bartolini and Medici families.*

ANDREA DELLA ROBBIA - *Bust of a child — Glazed Terracotta.*

MICHELANGELO — *Bacchus.*   DONATELLO — *St. John the Baptist.*   DONATELLO — *St. George.*

B. AMMANNATI — *Leda and the Swan.* ⬆
ANDREA DELLA ROBBIA — *Madonna and Child.*

◄

MICHELANGELO —
The Pitti Tondo, in which the figures of the Madonna, Child and St. John are harmoniously inserted, was sculpted in 1504 for Bartolomeo Pitti.

In Piazza dei Ciompi, where the Loggia del Pesce is located (originally built by Vasari in the old marketplace and recently reconstructed here), there is a characteristic antique market called the « Flea Market ».

►

110

THE CHURCH OF SANTA CRO-
CE (HOLY CROSS), *attributed to
Arnolfo di Cambio, is perhaps the
most beautiful Gothic church in
Italy, despite the fact that its
splendid simplicity and extreme
sobriety are contaminated by the
relatively modern façade, built by
Niccolò Matas (1854-1863) copying
the Tuscan Gothic style of the Cathedral of Florence. In the Basilica are the tombs of some of the
most famous personalities of Italian art, history and literature.*

BENEDETTO DA MAIANO — *Pulpit representing stories of the life of St. Francis (1475).* ➤

◄◄ **DONATELLO** — *Tabernacle of the Annunciation in grey stone with gilt highlights.*

◄◄ **BERNARDO ROSSELLINO** — *Tomb of Leonardo Bruni, which became a prototype for 15th century Florentine funeral monuments.*

113

GIOTTO — *Frescoes in the Bardi Chapel, painted in 1317 with Stories of the life of St. Francis. In the photo: The Funeral of St. Francis.*

114

In the silent and suggestive Cloister of Santa Croce is the PAZZI CHAPEL, original creation of Brunelleschi, which is preceded by an airy portico with 6 Corinthian columns. On the roof rises a low conical cupola which culminates in a graceful columned lantern.

In the museum of the OPERA DI SANTA CROCE some of the greatest masterpieces of Florentine art are displayed. Among these was an extremely valuable crucifix painted on wood by Cimabue, unfortunately badly damaged in the flood of 1966.

PIAZZALE MICHELANGELO — A fabulous spot with a world-famous view. We see the city divided by the river, with its series of fine bridges. In the square stands a monument to Michelangelo Buonarroti, with a copy of his David at the top, and with the four statues made for the tombs of Giuliano and Lorenzo de' Medici: Night, Day, Dawn and Dusk.

SAN MINIATO AL MONTE — The building was begun in the 11th century and took two centuries to complete. It is in the typically Florentine version of the Romanesque style. Like many other buildings in the city, it presents a clear disposition of spaces and of architectural masses, as well as a restrained, elegant decoration in marble of two colours. The façade, rhythmically divided by five wide, unencumbered arches, dates from the 12th century. In its upper part, the geometrical scheme is broken and the excessive detail partly destroys the harmony of the composition. The central mosaic shows Christ Blessing. At the top, the Eagle of the « Arte di Calimala » and Patron of the Church. To the right of the Basilica stands the Bishop's Palace, the summer residence of the Prelates of Florence. To the left stands the ancient Tower on which Michelangelo placed the cannons for the defence of Florence during the siege by the Imperial troops.

The interior is intimate and peaceful, adorned with a delicate decoration of many-coloured marbles, partly spoilt by a revetment of scagliola.

SAN MINIATO AL MONTE — The magnificent Pulpit of San Miniato is supported by the marble enclosure of the choir and 2 elegant columns. A small statue and the eagle of St. John the Evangelist hold the lecturn.

The simple CHURCH OF SAN SALVATORE AL MONTE, *that Michelangelo affectionately called « mia bella villanella » (my pretty country girl), is immersed in a beautiful setting of tall cypress trees. The actual construction, built on the site of a pre-existing Franciscan church, is by Cronaca.* ➤

The PORTA SAN NICCOLO' *and the hill that runs along the medieval walls and leads to the Fortress of Belvedere.* ➤

◄ A view of the enchanting and silent Via di San Leonardo, that winds its way through the olive groves of the hills of Arcetri.

FORT BELVEDERE — *Built by the architect Giovanni dei Medici and Bernardo Buontalenti. It was erected at the order of Ferdinand I; originally a fortress and later used as a barracks, it houses today various interesting art exhibition.* ▼

The NORTH FLORENCE EXIT of the HIGHWAY OF THE SUN - A 1 — The ultramodern church of St. John the Baptist on the Highway, made of stone and reinforced concrete whose overall structure brings to mild the form of a tent. Numerous contemporary art works, such as the bronze doors by P. P. Fazzini and other noteworthy religious paintings, mosaics and sculptures, enrich the interior.
The work was done by the architect Giovanni Michelucci.

CERTOSA DEL GALLUZZO - (Night View) — *From Gothic to neo-classic, this Monastery was founded in the 14th century by Niccolò Acciaiuoli, who donated the building and the hill on which it stands to the Carthusian monks. He established it when, together with other Florentine noblemen, he resolved to withdraw from public affairs in order to lead a hermit's life, far from the pomp of city life and the corruption of the world.*

FIESOLE — *A pictures-que View of this little town, situated on one of the loveliest hills around Florence. From Fiesole we get a pano-rama of the whole cir-cle of the surrounding hills, some of the most romantic in Italy.*

FIESOLE — *Roman Amphitheatre, dating to the 1st centuri B.C. Af-ter having been an im portant Etruscan cen-tre, the little town ca-me under the rule of Rome. It was the first nucleus.*

A beautiful panorama of FIESOLE with, in the foreground, the 13th century campani-le of the Cathedral made in the form of a tower.

124

FIESOLE — *The picturesque Church of St. Francis, built in 1330 on the top of a suggestive hill where once stood the Etruscan Acropolis, later the Roman and finally the Medieval strongholds.*

On the slopes of the Fiesolian hills, half way between Florence and Fiesole, the picturesque residential town of San Domenico rises in an ample and magnificent panorama of olive groves and cypresses.

FIESOLE — *The Cathedral: Built at the beginning of the 11th century and amplified in the successive centuries, it underwent extensive changes during the restoration of 1878, particularly on the façade.*

Foto Bazzechi

The following are some aspects of the most important traditional Florentine festivals. On Easter the colorful celebration of the « SCOPPIO DEL CARRO » takes place, which consists in the touching off of fireworks, contained in an enormous, decorated wooden cart, by means of a rocket shaped like a dove which slides along a wire connected to the high altar of the Cathedral. If the dove's journey to and from the altar is successful then the Florentines cheer it as a good omen for the harvest. On the feast of St. John the Baptist, patron saint of Florence, the characteristic football game in medieval costumes is held, preceded and followed by a parade with the marchers clothed in 15th century costumes.

Another holiday based on old tradition is the FESTA DEL GRILLO (Cricket hunt) that is held in the Cascine Park on Ascension Day.

Coat of Arms of the 21 Arts

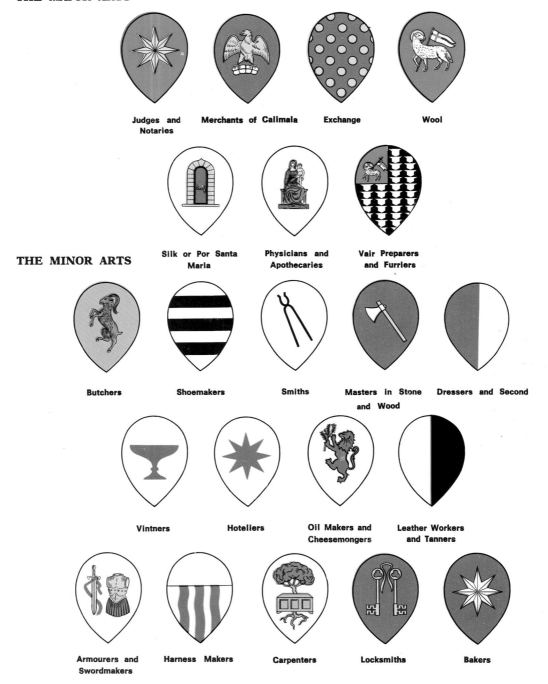

THE MAJOR ARTS

Judges and Notaries

Merchants of Calimala

Exchange

Wool

Silk or Por Santa Maria

Physicians and Apothecaries

Vair Preparers and Furriers

THE MINOR ARTS

Butchers

Shoemakers

Smiths

Masters in Stone and Wood

Dressers and Second

Vintners

Hoteliers

Oil Makers and Cheesemongers

Leather Workers and Tanners

Armourers and Swordmakers

Harness Makers

Carpenters

Locksmiths

Bakers

VF 2

L. 8000

I.V.A. compresa